Some Kids Are Deaf

by Lola M. Schaefer

Consulting Editor: Gail Saunders-Smith, Ph.D.

Consultant: Judith M. Gilliam
Member, Board of Directors
National Association of the Deaf

Pebble Books

an imprint of Capstone Press
Mankato, Minnesota

W9-APV-375

Pebble Books are published by Capstone Press,
151 Good Counsel Drive, P.O. Box 669, Mankato, Minnesota 56002.
www.capstonepress.com

1 2 3 4 5 6 06 05 04 03 02 01

Library of Congress Cataloging-in-Publication Data
Schaefer, Lola M., 1950–
    Some kids are deaf/by Lola M. Schaefer.
    p. cm.—(Understanding differences)
    Includes bibliographical references and index.
    Summary: Simple text and photographs describe the condition of deafness and
some of the everyday activities of children who are deaf.
    ISBN-13: 978-0-7368-0665-7 (hardcover)
    ISBN-10: 0-7368-0665-2 (hardcover)
    ISBN-13: 978-0-7368-8793-9 (softcover pbk.)
    ISBN-10: 0-7368-8793-8 (softcover pbk.)
    1. Deaf—Juvenile literature. 2. Deafness—Juvenile literature. [1. Deaf.
2. Physically handicapped.] I. Title. II. Series.
HV2380 .S3   2001
362.4'2—dc21   00-027222

Note to Parents and Teachers

The Understanding Differences series supports national social studies standards related to individual development and identity. This book describes children who are deaf and illustrates their special needs. The photographs support early readers in understanding the text. The repetition of words and phrases helps early readers learn new words. This book also introduces early readers to subject-specific vocabulary words, which are defined in the Words to Know section. Early readers may need assistance to read some words and to use the Table of Contents, Words to Know, Read More, Internet Sites, and Index/Word List sections of the book.

Table of Contents

Some kids are deaf. Kids who are deaf cannot hear.

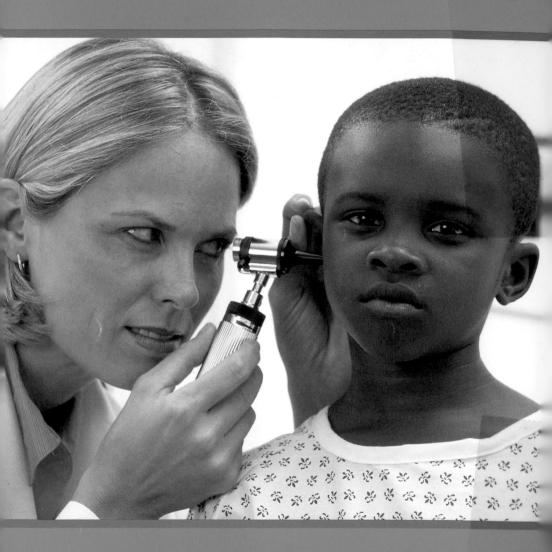

Some kids are deaf when they are born. Some kids become deaf from a sickness or from getting hurt.

Kids who are deaf depend on their sense of sight. Flashing lights tell them when it is time for class.

Some kids who are deaf use sign language. Sign language is hand movements that stand for numbers, letters, and words.

Some kids who are deaf use their voice to talk. A speech therapist teaches them to speak clearly.

Some kids who are deaf like to read. Saying the sounds helps them learn words.

Some kids who are deaf use a special telephone. They type messages on the machine to call friends.

closed captioning

Some kids who are deaf watch TV. Closed captioning appears on the bottom of the TV screen. The words tell what people on TV are saying.

Some kids who are deaf enjoy music. They can feel the vibrations.

Words to Know

communicate—to share information, ideas, or feelings with another person; people communicate by talking, writing, and using sign language.

deaf—being unable to hear; some kids who are deaf can hear some sounds; some kids who are deaf wear hearing aids or have cochlear implants to help them hear better.

speech therapist—a person who is trained to help people speak clearly

telephone—a machine that allows people to talk to others who are not close by; kids who are deaf use a teletypewriter that is added to a telephone; the teletypewriter lets them type a message; the message is then printed on the other person's machine.

vibrations—fast movements back and forth; musical instruments make vibrations when people play them.

Read More

Gordon, Melanie Apel. *Let's Talk About Deafness.* The Let's Talk Library. New York: Rosen, 1999.

Haughton, Emma. *Living with Deafness.* Austin, Texas: Raintree Steck-Vaughn, 1999.

Woolley, Maggie. *Being Deaf.* Think About. Mankato, Minn.: Smart Apple Media, 1999.

Internet Sites

FactHound offers a safe, fun way to find Internet sites related to this book. All of the sites on FactHound have been researched by our staff.

Here's how:

1. Visit *www.facthound.com*

2. Type in this special code **0736806652** for age-appropriate sites. Or enter a search word related to this book for a more general search.

3. Click on the **Fetch It** button.

FactHound will fetch the best sites for you!

Index/Word List

closed captioning, 19
flashing lights, 9
friends, 17
hear, 5
learn, 15
machine, 17
movements, 11
music, 21
read, 15
sickness, 7

sight, 9
sign language, 11
sounds, 15
speak, 13
speech therapist, 13
talk, 13
telephone, 17
TV, 19
vibrations, 21
voice, 13

Word Count: 158
Early-Intervention Level: 15

Editorial Credits
Mari C. Schuh, editor; Kia Bielke, designer; Katy Kudela, photo researcher

Photo Credits
Arthur Tilley/FPG International LLC, 6
Charles B. Smith/Deaf Native American Children, 4, 20
David F. Clobes, 18
Gregg R. Andersen, cover, 1, 8, 12, 14, 16
Kevin Vandivier, 10

Special thanks to the students and staff of the Minnesota State Academy for the Deaf in Faribault, Minnesota, for their assistance with this book.